Discovery KIDS™

TOTALLY GROSS

PaRragon

Bath · New York · Cologne · Melbourne · Delhi
Hong Kong · Shenzhen · Singapore

ACKNOWLEDGEMENTS

t = top, b = bottom, l = left, r = right, c = centre

Cover images courtesy of istockphoto.com and Shutterstock.com
4l Dragon _ fang/Dreamstime.com, 5r Nruboc/Dreamstime.com, 6tl sdominick/
istockphoto.com, 8tr Shell114/Shutterstock.com, 8cl princessdloft/istockphoto.com,
9tl Eleonora Kolomiyets/Shutterstock.com, 9br gorilla images/Shutterstock.com,
10–11 Shutterstock.com, 11tr tehcheesiang/Shutterstock.com, 12l Dreamstime.com,
13bl Bevan Goldswain/Shutterstock.com, 17tc Jubal Harshaw/Shutterstock.com,
19tc okili77/Shutterstock.com, 19bl Stuart Jenner/Shutterstock.com, 20–21
Dreamstime.com, 22bl SteveBower/Shutterstock.com

This edition published by Parragon Books Ltd in 2017 and distributed by
Parragon Inc.
440 Park Avenue South, 13th Floor
New York, NY 10016
www.parragon.com

ISBN 978-1-4748-7977-4

Printed in China

Contents

11 facts about SLIMY SNOT

The scientific word for nose-picking is **RHINOTILLEXOMANIA.**

#001

A person **swallows about a quart of snot** a day without even realizing it.

#002

Snot is made of **water, salt, and a gluey, sugary substance called mucin ...**

#003

... When the water dries out it turns into **hard boogers.**

#004

Snot moves through your breathing tubes at **half an inch per hour.** Bamboo grass grows more quickly than this.

#005

A sneeze hurtles out snot at over 37 MILES PER HOUR— that's faster than most New York subway trains. #006

The world sneezing record is held by British girl Donna Griffiths. She **SNEEZED A MILLION TIMES IN A ROW.** #007

If you've been hanging out in a **dusty room,** your snot will be a **GRAY dust-color.** #008

YOUR SNOT protects you from dirt and germs in the air by catching them. #010

Your snot looks more **yellow** when you have **a cold** because of all the **white blood cells** in it. #009

Snot is more than just sticky goo. It contains **antibodies** that help the body recognize **invading bacteria and viruses,** and creates **enzymes** to help kill them. #011

9 SLOBBERY SPIT FACTS

Your mouth produces between ONE AND TWO QUARTS OF SPIT (also known as saliva) a day.

#001

In some parts of the world, it is thought that a **mother's saliva can help build up a child's immune system**, so moms chew their babies' food before feeding it to them.

#002

Your saliva turns your food into a SOUP-LIKE MIXTURE, which makes it easier to swallow.

#003

Yawning really hard can make your spit spray **more than 3 feet.** This is called GLEEKING.

#004

In Singapore, you can be fined $1700 **for spitting in the street.**

#005

A single COW

makes as much **saliva as 200 HUMANS.** It helps them chew all that grass. #006

FULMAR CHICKS SPIT

at other animals to keep them away. #007

Llamas spit when they get annoyed. Their spit is super-smelly because it includes food from their stomach. #008

Spitting cobras spit painful venom **straight into the eyes of predators,** and then slither away to safety. #009

3 VILE VOMIT FACTS

Vomit is very **ACIDIC** and **dissolves your teeth.** #001

Vomit contains half-digested food and bits of stomach lining, which look like

lumps of carrot. #002

When one person vomits, it makes **everyone** around them feel sick, too. This can be useful if you've all eaten something **poisonous.** #003

5 SMELLY POO FACTS

Your poop smells because of stinky chemicals called **skatole** and **indole.**
#001

People **fart 14** times a day.
#002

Cabbage contains **stinky sulfur,** which gives you **smelly farts.**
#003

1/3 of your **poop** is made of bacteria.
#004

Corn passes straight through you, and comes out looking **EXACTLY THE SAME** as when it went in. This is because you cannot digest its tough, fibrous kernels.
#005

11 facts about PEE

When it first comes out, pee is **cleaner** than spit. #001

urine is **95** percent **water.** #002

The other 5 percent is old body cells, unwanted material from your food, and salt. #003

Ancient Egyptian doctors used to taste people's urine to find out if they were diabetic. #004

You pee between one and two litres of urine a day. #005

Some people think **drinking your own pee** makes you healthier. #006

Throughout your life, you pee about 45,000 quarts of urine.

That's enough to fill a small swimming pool. #007

Your pee is yellow because of a chemical called urochrome. #008

You can pee faster or slower by controlling the muscles underneath your bladder. #009

Male lobsters have bladders in their heads, and shoot pee at each other. #010

If you eat **asparagus**, your pee will smell of it. #011

11

5 Facts about Burping

Swallowing air as you eat and drink can make you **BURP and fart.** #001

Burping gets rid of a quart of gas from your **stomach** every day. #002

Drinking through a straw can **make you burp,** because you swallow more air. #003

In the zero gravity of space, **ASTRONAUTS WET BURP** because some of their stomach contents come out, too. #004

The **LOUDEST BURP** ever recorded was as loud as a **car alarm.** #005

8 BAD BACTERIA FACTS

Lots of bacteria live in your armpits and feet. They live off the sweat. #001

There are about 20,000 microbes (tiny bacteria) on every square inch of a desk. #003

A single ounce of fluid in your large intestine contains 35 trillion bacteria. #002

If you could get bacteria to line up in a row, 10,000 would fit across your fingernail. #004

A piece of chicken that is starting to smell is covered with at least 64 million bacteria per square inch. #005

Hot water is much better than cold water at getting rid of bacteria from your hands. Most bacteria are cooked by the heat. #006

A kitchen sink is home to 10,000 times more germs than a toilet. #007

One bacterium can turn into millions of bacteria in less than a day. #008

14

6 DEADLY DISEASE FACTS

The Black Death killed more than 25 million people across Europe, which was one-third of the population at the time.

#001

More than 220 million people around the world suffer from malaria each year.

#002

The plague germ was spread by rat fleas. It was called Yersinia pestis.

#003

On average, one person catches tuberculosis every 3.6 seconds.

#004

There can be as many as 5 billion viruses in one drop of blood.

#005

Smallpox killed 30 percent of the people who caught it.

#006

15

12 FACTS ABOUT PESKY PARASITES

The **average human** body carries between **2 and 5.5 lb** of parasitic bacteria (organisms that feed on a larger host).

#001

The largest parasitic worm ever found

was **28 inches** long. It was found living in a female sperm whale's womb.

#002

A tapeworm **can live inside a human gut** for up to 20 years. #003

Tiny **white pinworms** live in your gut, but move to your

BOTTOM

to lay eggs. #004

Parasitic worm eggs get into soil through animal droppings ... #005

... There can be **THOUSANDS** of parasitic worm eggs **in one handful of soil**. #006

Flukes are parasitic worms found in **FISH, CATTLE, AND SHEEP.** Humans can also become infected by swimming in fluke-infested water. #008

Hookworms can live in your intestine, sucking on **YOUR BLOOD.** #007

Humans can become infected with the parasite *Toxoplasma gondii* by eating undercooked meat, or coming into contact with **infected cat poo**. #009

Thorny-headed worms hatch inside pond crustaceans, which are then eaten by ducks. The worm reproduces inside the duck, and its **eggs come out in the duck's poop.** They are then eaten by a crustacean, and the cycle begins again. #010

A female flea sucks up to **15 TIMES** her own body weight in blood every day.

#011

The **tongue-eating** louse **EATS THE TONGUE** of its fish victim, and lives in its place. #012

17

12 facts about SURGERY

ANCIENT ROMANS
practiced plastic surgery to repair **noses**, **eyes**, **lips,** and **teeth**.

#001

Most surgeries in Renaissance times **(14th–17th centuries)** were performed in **BARBER SHOPS.**

#003

One procedure in **ancient Rome** was the removal of **scar tissue** from the back, because it implied that a man had **turned his back in battle** and was a

COWARD.

#002

Many of the patients seen by 16th-century Italian surgeon **GASPARE TAGLIACOZZI** were treated for wounds caused by **DUELS** or **STREET FIGHTS.**

#004

Tagliacozzi created **new noses** using **ARM TISSUE.**
However, the new nose could fall off if the person blew it too hard.

#005

Australian artist Stelios Arcadious had an **EAR** grown from cells in a laboratory implanted in his arm to make him a living art exhibit. #006

About **17 million** plastic surgery operations are carried out every year worldwide … #007

… More take place in SWITZERLAND than any other country, with about **216 procedures** per **100,000 people** each year. #008

In the Middle Ages, surgeons used **herbs** and **alcohol** as simple anesthetics. #009

The earliest form of surgery was **trepanning,** which involved cutting a small round hole in the head. #010

In 2007, a newspaper reported that a man in Colorado had his **THUMBS NARROWED** so that he could **use his iPhone more efficiently.** But the story turned out to be **fake**. #011

Some fashion-conscious women have a **toe bone removed** so that they can wear slim-flitting shoes. #012

19

9 facts about GARBAGE

Mumbai, India, gets rid of the horrible smell of its garbage dump by pouring **thousands of quarts of deodorant on it**.

#001

The **Citarum River** in Indonesia is full of the garbage of **9 million people** plus the liquid waste of **500 factories** ...

#002

... In places, the water can no longer be seen beneath the moving carpet of garbage ...

#003

...Boatmen still go on the river, but not to fish. **They look for things in the garbage to sell**.

#004

The Pacific is home to the **Great Pacific Garbage Patch,** a vast soup of debris and chemical sludge that covers about **2,000 square miles**.
#005

About **14 billion pounds of garbage** is dumped into the oceans every year, **most of it plastic**.
#006

When rubbish decomposes in a landfill, it produces methane gas—that's the smelly gas **in farts**.
#007

In a landfill, cigarette butts take 12 years to biodegrade. **"Disposable" diapers take 800 years** to biodegrade.
#008

Until the early 20th century, thrown-out food was mixed with **animal remains** to make a greasy gunk used in soaps and candles.
#009

11 GROSS FACTS ABOUT HOMES

Every time you flush the toilet, **you send an invisible 6-foot plume of bacteria** into the air that lands on exposed surfaces.

#001

The toilet is not the dirtiest place in the bathroom—

IT'S THE SINK. The sink has **130,000 germs** per square inch, but the toilet seat only has **120 germs per square inch.**

#002

People in Florida found that **Cuban tree frogs** had swum up their pipes into their toilet bowls.

#003

A kitchen chopping board has **200 percent** more bacteria than the average **toilet seat**. #004

Mice can squeeze through **cracks as small as 0.2 inch** to get into your house, and nest under the floor. #005

Brown rat droppings are like mouse poop, but **three times larger**. #006

Mouse droppings are easy to identify because they are **0.2 inch long, black,** and **shaped like grains of rice**. #007

Black rat droppings are more **sausage-shaped,** and look like fatter jelly beans. #008

Bat droppings look like mouse droppings but are **shiny, speckled,** and **always found in a pile**. #009

COCKROACH POOP looks like small dark specks. #011

Bird poop contains **acid,** which eats into house bricks and damages them. #010

INDEX